Seduction for Love

Seduction for Love

Naitian Wang, Ph.D.

University at Albany, State University of New York

ISBN: 1-4140-3033-9 (e-book)
ISBN: 1-4140-3032-0 (Paperback)

Library of Congress Control Number: 2003098662

This book is printed on acid free paper.

Printed in the United States of America
Bloomington, IN

1stBooks - rev. 11/17/03

To my father

Acknowledgement

The author wishes to thank Shari Goldberg. Ms. Goldberg has helped the author revise and edit this book. Her help has been invaluable.

Table of Contents

Preface
A Tale of the Author

The story really begins about one thousand years ago. It was a very prosperous time in the Chinese history and China was then called the Great Song. It was a time when resources were plenty and culture was blossoming. The most popular and prestigious form of literature was poetry. Nowadays, those works are known as classic Chinese poems and every schoolchild in China can recite some of them. Those poems had very strict formats and strict rules for selecting words. Authors had to convey appealing messages without violating the rules and formats. When a poem was well-written, the rules and formats actually made the message more appealing, more beautiful, and more elegant.

At that time, there was a poet named Ying Liu who was famous for writing romantic and seductive poems. When he was young, in one of his poems, he wrote "disregard those meaningless high-ranked official titles, go write and read some romantic poems." Later on, he took the civil imperial examination, which was the only way people could get appointed to high-ranked offices. He scored high and was called upon to meet the emperor. The emperor had heard about him, had read his poems, and had been quite annoyed by his liberalism and arrogance. The emperor said to Ying Liu: "Why don't you just disregard those meaningless high-ranked official titles, go write some romantic poems?" Ying Liu then was not appointed to any office and spent his whole life writing poems. In history he was, therefore, known as "the poem-writer with an edict", meaning that he proudly obeyed the emperor's edict to be a full-time poem-writer.

Near the northern border of Great Song (i.e., China), there was a smaller country named Jin. One day, the king of Jin was reading a poem written by Ying Liu. In that poem, Ying Liu described the beauty and prosperity of a town in the south of China. After reading that poem, the king of Jin suddenly had an urge to invade the Great Song and he did. After a couple of years, Jin conquered Great Song. This was probably just a legendary tale. However, it surely indicates how wonderful and powerful people think Ying Liu's poems are.

The problem, however, was that no one could support himself by just writing poems. Poets generally had other means making money (most of the poets were appointed officials). Ying Liu, however, managed to survive with his beautiful poems and his natural ability with women. When he died poorly, more than two hundred beautiful courtesans who loved him dearly arranged his funeral and buried him. It was said that, for several years, each day there were women crying or reciting his poems near his grave.

One thousand years later, a boy was born into a Wang family in Shandong province, northeast of China. He was given a name of Naitian. When he went to school, his teachers were surprised by how easy it was for him to interpret those classic Chinese poems that had been written in ancient Chinese language. Especially with Ying Liu's poems, he understood and recited them as if he had known them all along. He started writing classic Chinese poems beautifully in the same style as Ying Liu. At the age of twelve, people around him were convinced that he was reincarnated from Ying Liu.

Before Naitian was born, the communists had taken over. China was quite a different country now. It was the period of the well-known "Great Cultural Revolution Movement" when he went to elementary school. It was a period of time when everything was political and when artists, scientists, and technicians were forced to become physical laborers. However, that little boy in a remote countryside village showed no interest in anything political and had a persistent admiration of arts, poetry, and science. He was the first person from that area of more than six villages to go to college, and that remained the case for the next three years.

Naitian attended East China Normal University at Shanghai, the biggest city of China, studying psychology. College was a relatively relaxing period, during which he further explored his interest in poetry. Despite his brightness and talents, Naitian had a hard time with women. Under the communist control at that time, dating was not allowed for middle school and high school students. His natural instinct with women had not been nurtured. He found himself quite clumsy when interacting with women. Yet with a poetic soul, he easily fell in love with those beautiful women around him. There were many failures in his attempt attracting women. Each was painful and frustrating.

On one summer vocation, Naitian went back to his hometown. He talked with his father who had never gone to school in his entire life and did not know how to read and write a single word. His father was surprised.

"I thought you are learning psychology," he said, "how come you do not know what those women were thinking."

"Psychology is not about mind-reading," Naitian explained.

His father seemed disappointed and left. Naitian started to think that psychology probably should study something more useful. There must be methods that could work for attracting women and those methods should be discovered. He tried to analyze his past experiences and was able to draw a couple of conclusions.

From that day on, Naitian has never stopped his search for seduction strategies. Gradually he had more and more successes while less and less failures. In the end, whenever he loved someone, he could generally have her love him. For Ying Liu, it was his natural instincts that worked well when attracting women. For Naitian, he had to discover the nature of those natural instincts and develop them into more concrete methods. When he worked at a university counseling center, Naitian helped many students with their love relationships.

In the fall of 1997, Naitian came to the United States for his doctoral study in the area of counseling psychology. He quickly searched the database of APA (i.e., American Psychological Association) journals but did not find any useful study or theory on seduction. However, during the course of his doctoral study, he found that findings in many areas could be used for seduction. Some findings have drawn conclusions that are in perfect agreement with the seduction strategies he had discovered before he came to the United States, while others have refined them.

Naitian has thought about writing and revealing his seduction secrets. However, during his clinical practice, Naitian has seen many deceptions and betrayals in relationships and has seen how painful it was for those who were hurt in their relationships. People often made others believe that they loved them when they actually did not, as a result of which they left those victims with endless pain and endless doubts in trusting another person. If he revealed his seduction strategies, Naitian was afraid that people might use them for no good.

On one summer weekend, Yuhua, Naitian's beautiful wife, was very excited. "I've got to go to the laboratory tonight. Can you go with me?" she asked. "Sure," Naitian replied. Yuhua works in a big drug company as a microbiologist. It was not uncommon for her to go and do a little bit work during weekends. A better agent treating cancer had been discovered for a while. However, no drug company could manufacture it because the productivity was too low. Whoever manufactured it would lose money. The main focus of Yuhua's lab, and many other labs, was on how to increase productivity.

In the laboratory, Yuhua pointed to a sharp curve on the computer screen, "This can be a big breakthrough."

"Look at this curve," Yuhua continued, "If it reaches 2000, our company will be able to manufacture the drug."

Yuhua and Naitian waited and the curve slowly reached 2000. The curve continued going up until it reached 2200. Yuhua was thrilled, "before, the best we could do was 1400."

Naitian was equally excited and asked, "What did you do differently this time?"

"I used a new mutant," Yuhua replied proudly. What she meant was that she had changed part of a microorganism's gene, created and used a new strain.

That night, Yuhua was too excited to fall asleep. So was Naitian. However, what went through Naitian's mind was quite different. Naitian was thinking about the seduction strategies he had discovered. Everyone has the potential of love. Love is in everyone's blood. Yet, people can not fulfill their potential of love if they do not know how. When you love someone, you want that someone to love you back. With good strategies, you can earn someone's love. With poor strategies, you can only earn rejections. With painful experiences of rejections in the past, people do not dare to love anymore. The world would be a much better place if people were able to fulfill their dreams of love. Love is like a psychological agent that can make people's lives happy and healthy. Seduction strategies are like the appropriate mutant that enables love to be fulfilled. "I will tell people how to use the most productive mutant," Naitian said to himself. It was that night that Naitian decided to write this book and call it "Seduction for Love".

May God bless those who dare to love.

Chapter One

The Goal of Seduction

Seduction occurs in almost every romantic relationship. Only when two people start to love each other at exactly the same minute, is there a possibility that seduction may not occur. When a man starts to love a woman earlier than the woman starts to love him, he naturally tries to seduce her either intentionally or unintentionally, either skillfully or unskillfully, and either successfully or unsuccessfully. The above is also true if a woman starts to love a man earlier than the man starts to love her. This book is just trying to show you how to seduce the one you love intentionally, skillfully, and successfully.

Seduction happens everywhere. Seduction can serve many purposes. Usually people use this term to define any activity or intention to make a targeted person more approachable sexually or romantically. One form that most people are familiar with is flirtation. Flirtation is a kind of behavior to convey your sexual interest, to evoke the other person's sexual desire in general, and to bring up the other person's sexual interest in you in particular.

Flirtation can be viewed as one specific technique in the process of seduction. In this book, seduction is defined as the process of obtaining another person's feeling of romantic love for you. The ultimate goal is to make your targeted person (very often I will call that person "your potential lover") love you, which generally would lead to a long-term romantic relationship or marriage.

While sex can be part of the process and outcome, gaining sexual pleasure is not the direct goal of the seduction strategies described in this book. Because romantic love usually, although not always, involves sexual pleasure, seduction strategies described in this book may be used to gain sexual pleasure. However, if sexual pleasure is all you want, you may find that the seduction strategies in this book are not very cost-effective. You may find that you have done too much work for something that you could have gotten easily. You are, therefore, advised to use more simple and easy methods to pursue your sexual pleasure.

Sexual pleasure itself is beautiful and pure sexual pleasure may be your goal when you are not ready for a love relationship. For those who are not ready for a love relationship, a love relationship can, at times, damage their experience and enjoyment of sexual pleasure. Also, both people can get hurt if pure sexual pleasure is what you want and yet you have made the other person fall in love with you. Again, it is not a good idea to use this book if your interest at this point is just sexual pleasure.

As was said earlier, the goal of seduction in this book is to make your potential lover love you. Caution is warranted here. Many people want to be loved romantically or non-romantically. Generally, being loved makes people feel good and worthwhile. Many people, therefore, are in constant need of being loved. Many people enjoy the feeling of being loved more than enjoy the feeling of loving others. While it is a normal phenomenon in our society, if you are kind of extreme with this regard, where you only enjoy the feeling of being loved and seldom enjoy the feeling of loving others, you are advised to see a psychologist. Chapter Three will address this issue briefly and may help you learn how to love others. It is an important issue because as a precondition to launch the process of seduction for love, you should have developed romantic feelings for your targeted person.

There are three reasons for this precondition. The first is an ethical one. In any romantic relationship, love should be reciprocal. It is just selfish and harmful to make someone love you when you do not love him or her. The second is a practical one. The process of seduction for love, at times, can be really hard work. Without your love for him or her, you will likely find that you can not carry it out.

The third reason is also a practical one. Seduction strategies in this book are not a guarantee of success in obtaining love for you with everyone. You will need to give up your pursuit at an appropriate point of time so that either of you will not get hurt psychologically. At the beginning, it is your love for her that motivates and sustains your pursuit. Gradually, you may find that your stay in the course of pursuit is more for wining than for love. That is, your competitiveness for wining the game has become the primary force that sustains your pursuit and your love for her has become the secondary force. When that happens, it is the appropriate point of time to quit your pursuit.

As an effort to make this book easier to read and write, I will write in a way that a male reader is assumed. For example, very often I will say "her romantic feelings for you develop" instead of "his or her romantic feelings for you develop". Please be advised that all statements are true for both genders, unless otherwise specified. Seduction strategies described in this book are effective both when a woman tries to attract a man and when a man tries to attract a woman.

Everyone is different. Every situation is different. Therefore, every course of seduction is different. However, for a perfect seduction, the following course is recommended.

Step 1. You shall love her

If you do not love her, please do not do anything seductive. You may succeed, but your success may get you into trouble. Psychologically, what you will lose may be far more than what you will gain.

Step 2. You shall make her love you

This is the most important part and it is the key phase of seduction. The most common mistake is to tell her that you love her to start the process of seduction. You shall lead her to develop romantic love for you before she ever knows that you have romantic feelings for her.

Step 3. You shall make her express her feelings for you

Under rare circumstance, you may want to tell her that you have feelings for her before she tells you that she has romantic feelings for you to speed up the process. Doing that, however, will compromise your future enjoyment of the relationship. For a perfect seduction, you shall wait for her to tell you that she loves you first.

Step 4. You shall accept her love

When she expresses her feelings for you, you shall accept her love immediately. Playing hard-to-get will damage your enjoyment of a future relationship.

Step 5. You shall work with her to make the relationship work

You may enjoy her love now. However, please remember to make efforts to build and improve your relationship with her. Otherwise, you may love each other but cannot enjoy the love.

Step 6. You shall dance her to the end of love

It is a fact that love may die. You shall work with her to end the relationship gracefully at an appropriate point of time. Success in ending a relationship gracefully will enable you and her to pursue and enjoy love with someone else more easily.

Chapter Two

The Process of Falling in Love

Because our goal of seduction is to make your targeted person, the one you fall in love with, to fall in love with you, we first need to understand how individuals fall in love. To better understand how people fall in love, I would like to ask you to think about your first love experience (if you have experienced one already). The first love experience is the most natural and uncontaminated love experience. After the first love experience, people generally have tried to use their cognition to interfere with their natural process of falling in love. The experiences after the first one, therefore, are less natural, more complex, and psychologically contaminated. If you observe a first love experience, the natural process of falling in love is plain to see.

In a broad sense, everyone is self-centered by nature. Our mind gathers information based on our sensors. Our sensors sense stimuli that are most relevant to us. Our feelings, thoughts, and actions are all based on the interpretation of the information we gathered. The feelings are what "I" feel. The thoughts are what "I" think. The actions are what "I" want to do. In our everyday lives, everything is about "I" or "me". I have friends because "I feel" that I like them. I avoid certain people because "I feel" that I do not like them. I eat because "I feel" hungry. I sleep because "I feel" tired. I argue with you because "I think" I am right. Our mind is consistently and primarily focused on "I" or "me". "I" or "me" is where our attention primarily focuses on.

Most people are able to give some of their attention to other people to understand what other people feel. When that happens, those behaviors are praised as caring and loving. However, there are individuals who seem unable to ever divert their attention from themselves to other people. Those individuals are generally described as egocentric, narcissistic, and uncaring. People naturally avoid being around those individuals because of their inability to care or to love.

When people start to fall in love, their attention gradually switches from themselves to their lovers. Their focus is not only on themselves any more. As they are falling deeper in love, people give more and more attention to their lovers. They pay more and more attention to what the other one is doing or is feeling. When people are absolutely in love, their focus is only on their lovers. They do not care about themselves any more. They only care about the other one. They have lost themselves and they are lover-centered. They feel that they are just their lovers' followers or satellites.

Some people argue that the totally lover-centered state is not a state of love. They argue that it is rather an infatuation. Some "mature" people try to disregard infatuation and remove it from the category of love. Believe it or not, it is an extreme state of love and it is also the most enjoyable state of love, in which "I" has lost its own entity and follows another entity completely. It is, fundamentally, similar to extreme religious feelings, in which people completely give themselves to God and totally believe that God is giving the best lives to them. It is more enjoyable than using psychotropic drugs, in which people only follow the flow of their feelings.

The only reason why some "mature" people disregard that state as love is simply because in that state they find that they have lost control over themselves, have behaved irrationally, have endangered themselves of being misled, and most importantly have been deeply hurt when their lovers left them. All in all, they are scared. After a failed love experience, people either disbelieve in "love" completely or redefine "love" to exclude the real thing. After all, locating our attention primarily on ourselves is a precondition for our self-protection and our survival. Switching our attention onto someone else makes us vulnerable. When objectively observed by a third party, however, the period of time when people are in the state of "infatuation" is probably the happiest period of time in their lives.

The process of falling in love is actually the process of switching our focus and attention from ourselves to another person. Our minds change from a self-centered state to a lover-centered state. In situations when love is reciprocal, both lovers take care of each other, put the other one ahead of themselves, and enjoy the presence of the other person. Gradually, it develops into a state that the center is neither one of them. Rather, the center is both of them. A new entity is formed by melting both individuals together. The focus, attention, and concern are the whole of the both rather than each individual. The new melted entity is more important than either one of them. "Team" is the word people often use to define a healthy relationship, in which both lovers have become one unit. This new unit's life then becomes the most primary. Sometimes, people have no feeling of one's own life at all. Rather, they only feel the feeling of that one unit's life.

When you fall in love with her, you lose your sense of yourself. You primarily focus on her. To make her fall in love with you, first you need to make her switch her primary attention from focusing on herself to focusing on you. Gradually, you need to make her lose her sense of herself and locate her primary attention on you. Then, willingly and happily, both of you work together and form a new entity that both of you will focus on.

Before proceeding onto how to make that switch of attention occur, the next two chapters are designed to help you psychologically prepare yourself before starting your seduction process.

Chapter Three

Psychological Preparation I

In the following two chapters we will discuss some basic issues about love and romance. Many people have initially learned about love and romance from movies and stories in their childhood. As beautiful as those stories may be, there is little truth in them. As they grow up, people then have learned about love and romance from their own past experiences, which are all circumstantial and therefore are very likely to lead to biased conclusions. This chapter and the next chapter are designed to correct some of the wrong notions about love and romance.

We will discuss resistances and obstacles for people falling in love. First, it will help you understand what you are going to deal with in the process of seduction because your potential lover may have those resistances. Second, it will help you overcome those resistances in you that have prohibited you from falling in love and therefore your ability to love will be enhanced. As discussed before, it is recommended that you love her first before you start to make her love you. In the end (after the next chapter), you will have an appropriate state of mind when you start your pursuit of love and romance.

In many societies, the sentence "Michael is rejected by Jen" has an implicit message, which is that Michael is not as good as Jen. Among youngsters, it is more obvious. It is not uncommon to hear them saying, "Kim is the most beautiful girl in our class and Jason wants to be her boyfriend. Isn't that funny? He must not know how fat he is." Many societies somehow make those who love but not be loved back look pathetic and less worthwhile. To avoid being looked at as the less worthwhile one, some people prefer "reject him or her first before he or she rejects you" and others have learned not to start loving someone unless that someone has fallen in love with them already.

This association between love and worth probably can be traced to animal mating behaviors. The strongest and most aggressive male is usually the most wanted by females and often ends up with the best female(s). In human world, people often rate males with beautiful girlfriends more competent, both in general and in unrelated areas, than they really are in comparison to other males.

In the process of an individual's socialization, the association between love and worth has been internalized into his or her mind. As a result, to love but not to be loved back is often associated with shame. Plus, people experience a strong feeling of being the underdog when falling in love (see Chapter Five). On the other hand, those who are loved but do not love in return feel quite proud and satisfied. Because of this pattern, many people are very resistant to fall in love, especially those who have been rejected cruelly in the past.

The feeling of shame in a situation where you love her and she does not love you prevents you from daring to develop romantic love freely. This feeling of shame is based on the association between love and worth. However, the association between love and worth is a bias. In our human world, it is really hard to evaluate an individual's worth. There are so many aspects that can be evaluated and everyone can have their own subjective evaluating system. Also, an individual's development of romantic love for another individual is not completely parallel to his or her evaluation of worth. It is not uncommon for a woman to give a high rating on someone's social worth and yet never fall in love with that person.

To love means you are ready to give your love to someone. Giving should never be associated with shame. One the other hand, if you only want to be loved and do not want to love, you simply just want to receive but not to give. When you are ready and willing to give your love to her, you should be proud of yourself because you are able to love and want to love. The fact that she does not love you should never make you less proud of yourself. You need a bigger heart to love than to receive love. To love is a more invaluable attribute in any society than wanting to be loved.

Being proud of yourself to love her will prepare your state of mind to facilitate your seduction, whereas feeling shame to love her will impede your seduction. The reason is simple. If you feel that you are doing something great, you are more likely to work hard and effectively.

Some people do not have the ability to love. Extremely egocentric individuals cannot love others and that is why people do not like to be around them. Other individuals' ability to love was impaired by their painful experiences of the past. They might have been deeply hurt by someone they loved or by everyone they had fallen in love with. Just imagine how it feels if you are near a snake shortly after you have been bitten by a poisonous snake and almost have lost your life.

In many cases, the hurt from a love relationship can be more deadly than a rattler's bite. As described in Chapter Two, when people are deeply in love, they have forgotten themselves completely and only focus on their lovers. Their lives have been all about their lovers and their relationships. All of a sudden, their lovers told them to stay away as if they are nothing but a pain in the neck. How do they start to lead their lives again? Many unhealthy breakups lead to depression and suicide. It would be cruel to expect those individuals to be able to love again in any short period of time.

Generally most people can recover from their negative experiences after a certain period of time. But it is very natural to lose the ability to love temporarily. It is also true that some people will never recover and will never be able to love again without adequate professional help.

To avoid being deeply hurt from a love relationship, many people have chosen not to love again. Some people think that they have "matured" not to fall in love. Some people think that they have "matured" to love in a different way, in which they will primarily pay attention to themselves in a relationship. As a matter of fact, they are just scared to really fall in love again. However, no one can blame them after what they have been through.

But falling in love is such a beautiful thing. People have an innate need to love and to be loved. To give up love in such a way is like to give up food after having had a choking experience. There are many ways to overcome resistance to love and to enhance an individual's ability to love.

First, be wise when ending a love relationship. The best scenario is a mutual breakup, in which both people come up with the conclusion that love has died between them. This usually happens when both lovers have really good communication in their relationship. Enhancing communication is not only a key element for maintaining a love relationship, as we all have learned, but also it is a key element for a good breakup. An individual's future ability to love will not be damaged after a healthy breakup. In many scenarios, one person wants to end a love relationship while the other wants to save the relationship. Most people only pay attention to how painful and hurtful the one who still wants the relationship (the victim) feels. Actually, it can equally damage the one who wants to end the relationship. It is very painful for many people to see themselves hurting the one whom they once deeply loved.

In those situations, an open discussion between the ex-lovers may help. Discussion should be as open, straightforward, and comprehensive as possible. Discussion should include both positive and negative experiences of the past. What have you enjoyed the most? What have you disliked? Discussion should not focus on what type of person (i.e., personalities) each one was. Rather, discussion should focus on what each one had done (i.e., behaviors) that made the good and the bad happen. It is more constructive to discuss behaviors than personalities. It is quite easy to get into a game of blaming each other when facing a breakup. But remember, two people who are both perfect do not necessarily have a good love relationship together. It is rare that a person would intentionally hurt someone he or she has loved.

A good discussion will help both individuals learn from that past experience and make them better lovers in the next relationship. A good discussion also will be able to give both individuals a sense of closure. Lacking a sense of closure generally locks psychological energy, causes anxiety, and prevents individuals from starting a new relationship whole-heartedly.

Under rare circumstances, it is impossible to get closure. For example, one of the lovers has suddenly stopped all means of communication without giving any explanation. Also, an ill-conducted discussion can not serve people well in terms of getting closure. Some people still experience unwanted and intrusive thoughts about their ex-lovers even several years after the breakup. It seems that they can not let their ex-lovers go. When people feel that they have been deeply hurt by someone, it is hard to let it go. If they can not let their ex-lovers go, they can not let the hurt go. They were hurt then and they are still hurt now. The hurt stays with them all along and they can feel the pain from time to time. If you are in this situation, you need to do something about it. You can not pursue a new love whole-heartedly with that hurt inside you.

An exercise of internal dialogue might help. Take one or two hours of your time. Find a quiet place. Have an internal conversation with that person. Tell what you want to tell that person in a way that is both sincere and constructive. Tell that person how he or she has hurt you. Tell that person how it feels then and since. Tell that person the pain has been with you for so long. Tell that person that now you want to let it go.

That person physically is not near you, but you have allowed him or her to stay in your psychological reality. You have allowed him or her to stay in your life and to continue hurting you. Now it is time to let him or her dissipate completely. Tell yourself that you are becoming a new person and you are no longer the one who has a broken heart. You are becoming a new person who will love proudly and be loved happily.

You may want to do this exercise several times. This generally should help. If this excise is not enough, consider seeking some professional help. After all, you deserve to love and to be loved.

In your future course of pursuing love and romance, learn to enjoy the pure feeling of "to love". To love should be a very pleasant feeling by itself. An individual who has matured enough generally is able to enjoy the pure feeling of "to love" without an expectation of being loved back. Enjoy the love that is inside you. Enjoy the feeling of wanting to care about another wonderful human being. Enjoy the very presence of a beautiful creature and never having to wonder how she might feel about you. "To love" itself should be able to make you feel happy.

Chapter Four

Psychological Preparation II

The previous chapter has discussed resistances to love and ways to overcome them. This chapter will discuss more general topics that are confusing to youngsters. However, adults may also find it helpful reading this chapter, as we all once were youngsters.

Many youngsters fall in love easily for the first time because they have not had a painful experience to impede them from doing so. Many youngsters tell their potential lovers directly without identifying any clue that their potential lovers are interested in them. It very likely leads to a total rejection. This first rejection is very painful. Some youngsters then realize that love does not happen simply by telling someone that they love her or by asking her to love back. Others are more persistent by continuously telling her how much they love her and how great it would be if they are together. Eventually, most youngsters have learned that persuading someone to love them is quite impossible.

Those innocent mistakes can lead to a great deal of frustration, especially as many youngsters feel that there is only one person whom they can love. Some adults still feel that there is only one person whom they can love. However, most adults feel that there are several people they can fall in love with. It is a matter of how person-specific romantic love is. Some people hold a mysterious belief that God only creates one person as their other half. It is a notion that romantic love happens in an extremely person-specific way. Others believe that there are certain types of people they can love. That is, they can fall in love with people who possess certain traits or a combination of traits. This is a notion that romantic love happens in a roughly person-specific way. The notion that romantic love happens in a person-specific way, either extremely or roughly, is widespread. Most adults entertain the notion that romantic love happens in a roughly person-specific way, whereas most youngsters entertain the notion that love happens in an extremely person-specific way.

It is true that romantic love happens in a person-specific way. However, that is not the whole story. Romantic love also develops in a situation-specific way. That is, for two given people, under one circumstance, romantic love may occur, whereas under a different circumstance romantic love may not occur. It is a common knowledge, for example, that it is easier to develop romantic feelings when people are traveling. In ordinary everyday life, people have a stable state of mind with their daily routine. When traveling, an individual's preset state of mind changes because everything is now different. Their minds are in a transitional state that is more open to exciting ideas.

An individual's state of mind determines the likelihood of whether or not romantic feelings would emerge. If two individuals meet in a sweaty summer afternoon and both of them are exhausted by heat, it is quite unlikely for them to develop romantic love. However, if they meet in a breezy, moonlighted, summer night dance party where romantic music is playing, it would be more likely for them to develop romantic feelings.

Some situations set an individual's mind into a state that is more open to romantic ideas. People often talk about moments. That is, sometimes two individuals suddenly feel that something special is going on. If they have failed to grasp the moment, they may never feel the same way again. Romantic love would just have sneaked away.

Romantic love is situation-specific and moment-specific. The underlying nature is that romantic love is state-of-mind-specific. The external stimuli primed an individual's state of mind and the construct of romantic love was activated and become accessible. This issue will be further discussed in Chapter Eight.

According to the fact that romantic love can happen when an individual has the appropriate state of mind, it seems that any given two individuals may fall in love if their states of mind are set to the appropriate state in a given moment. Well, that is probably too extreme to be true. It seems more likely that romantic love occurs both person-specifically and state-of-mind-specifically. However, one condition (i.e., the right person or the right state of mind) can compensate for the other. Romantic love does happen when one condition is weak while the other condition is strong enough.

Youngsters should remember that love can happen more easily than you think. Most likely, your first love will not be your last one. So open your mind and expect a new love if you are rejected by your first potential lover or if your first love relationship fails. Now it is a time to learn to love back those who are already in love with you. Give yourself and the one who loves you a chance and love may grow brightly. In other words, try to accept an offer of romantic love. It will be a good opportunity to learn how to love, how it feels to be loved, and how it is to be in a relationship. Any relationship is a learning opportunity. As people say, "a woman is a university". After being with a woman in a love relationship, you will become more mature and you will turn into a man who is more desirable and attractive.

For adults who are unable to love, as discussed in the previous chapter, professional help is suggested. Some people, however, have tried everything without success in recovering from a painful past. At this point, you may also try to accept an offer of romantic love. By doing that, you are giving the individual who loves you a chance to either fulfill their dreams or disillusion their dreams. You are doing them a favor if you give them a chance to know that they are in love with the wrong person. In some cases, they may be willing to nurture your ability to love, and you may be able to learn and love them.

Chapter Five

The Underdog Fairy Tales

As discussed in Chapter Two, the process of falling in love is actually the process of switching from a self-centered state to a lover-centered state. Therefore, to seduce her to fall in love with you, your job is to make her attention focus on you. Her sense of self will no longer exist. Rather, her sense is all centered to you. You will replace herself as her primary focus and concern. The question is how you are going to do that.

Many books and many movies tell stories about romance and love. As a matter of fact, it is not easy to find stories that do not involve romance and love nowadays. While some of those romantic stories are really moving, they do not offer much about how and why romance and love really happens. Romance and love seem to have come out of the blue in those stories. When I was in college, I read many books, trying to figure out how people fall in love. Many stories I read did confirm the process of falling in love that I have described in Chapter Two, yet no story gave me a clue of how the switch of focus occurs until one beautiful summer night.

That summer night, I was watching the movie *Sabrina* starring Harrison Ford. It was a story about a poor girl who fell in love with a romantic and wealthy man her family worked for. She usually climbed over a tree, watching their family's fancy parties and watching the man playing around with other women. She went to Paris and there was not a day that she forgot that man. She came back, a beautiful grown-up woman. She immediately attracted the man she secretly loved for all those years. In the end, she and that man' brother fell in love with each other. That man's brother was more able and more committed to

34

her. I found myself emotionally engaged with that movie. When she missed the man, I felt sad for her. When she was able to attract that man, I felt excited for her. When she got what she wanted, I felt thrilled for her. I went for a walk after the movie. I suddenly realized that I actually identified myself with her during that whole time. I felt whatever she was supposed to feel when the story unfolded.

That was interesting. I was excited by this realization. Probably most people would identify themselves with that girl when they were watching the movie. What does that mean? In that love story, that girl was an underdog who finally achieved her goal. Do people identify themselves with the underdog in love stories?

I then thought of those popular fairy tales. Cinderella and Snow White were two fairy tales that have survived from generation to generation. Everyone loves them. When people read the stories or see the movies, most likely they identify themselves with Cinderella or Snow White, the underdogs. In love situations, do people generally feel like the underdogs?

I then thought about my feelings toward a woman during the period of time when I fell in love with her. I admired her, her personality and her beauty. The feeling was like she was a queen and I was a servant. Definitely I felt like the underdog and she was the top-dog.

I was excited by this line of reasoning. When you fall in love with her, you feel that you are the underdog. But you cannot make her also feel that you are the underdog. No one falls in love romantically with an underdog. Only if you are the top-dog in her mind, can she fall in love with you. Before that man's brother fell in love with Sabrina, the brother was no longer a top-dog in his own mind. Sabrina had made him feel that what he had was meaningless and his life was not fulfilling at all. The reason is simple. If her attention is primarily on one entity (i.e., herself), to switch her attention to another entity (i.e., you), the other entity has to be more enticing than the previous one. An underdog is not more enticing than a top-dog.

The most common mistake in seduction is due to the fact that you have felt that you are the underdog.

When that message of how you feel is conveyed to her and if she is convinced, you will lose your chance completely. Very commonly, you tell her that you love her to start the pursuit. Then you try to tell her how much you love her to continue the pursuit. During this process, you would very often tell her how good you feel she is. While it feels nice to hear good words from other people, you are actually making her feel more and more that she is the top-dog. When that process continues much longer, your pursuit for love actually turns into an underdog's begging for love from a top-dog. If you continue to beg after you are told consistently to back off, you evoke a feeling of disdain from her. No romantic love can ever be possible then.

To make her feel that she is the underdog is not an evil idea. When you fall in love with her, you feel that you are the underdog already. To make her feel that she is an underdog is just to make her feel the same way as how you have been feeling and therefore is a fair game. To make her feel that she is an underdog is the toughest job because you surely do not want to make her feel that you look down on her. Some subsequent chapters will deal with this issue. For now, you need to remember that you should try to avoid making her feel that you are the underdog.

It is, however, possible that you can have a relationship with her when she feels that you are the underdog. It is also possible that the relationship can last. It occurs when some of her primary needs are fulfilled by being with you. Details will not be discussed in this book because it is not a preferable condition for you. It is not a preferable condition because you will feel that she has settled for you. It would be really hard, if not impossible, to feel that she is infatuated with you.

Now, do you know why being rejected is so devastating? Well, when you fall in love with someone, you feel that you are the underdog already. Being rejected makes you a worthless underdog, an under-underdog, or not a dog at all. When you are rejected, we all know that your primary feeling is "worthlessness". If you had had felt that you were the top- dog to begin with, being rejected probably would not have done much harm to you.

Actually, the fact that you feel yourself as the underdog and your potential lover as the top-dog can be easily confirmed in love poems. Most poems describe the authors' lovers or potential lovers as the top-dog. The authors generally put themselves in an underdog position. A nicer word for the feeling from an underdog toward a top-dog is "admiration". When you fall in love with your lover, you admire your lover's beauty, talents, personality, or whatever, either consciously or subconsciously. In the Chinese language, the word "love" generally is followed by the word "admiration" when used for romantic love (i.e., "the feeling of love" in Chinese is said as "ai mu zhi qing", literally "the feeling of love and admiration").

To clarify, the feeling of being the underdog is a psychological reality. It is not the objective reality. A higher ranked position socially does not necessarily make you a top-dog in her mind. The most crucial is that in her psychological reality, you are the top-dog. Something that has little meaning for you (or other people) can make you the top-dog in her mind. The next chapter will discuss more on this issue.

For an individual to fall in love, feeling like an underdog is the first step. Many youngsters know that fact by their instinct and they typically try to assume a top-dog role to attract the other person. When they want to attract a girl's attention, their spontaneous behavior is showing off. Many adults still have that tendency when they try to attract a woman. Yet, showing off is not as effective as expected, and it may do more harm than good in many situations. It may bring up a feeling of competition. It may also make her feel that your have hurt her self-esteem. The best way to make your potential lover feel like an underdog is mirroring. Discussion follows in the next chapter.

Chapter Six

Mirroring

My father was a farmer (I love that man!). I did some physical work with him when I was young. It always made me nervous when working with him because my father was a very strict man with an impatient temper. A small mistake or a slow action would lead him to react. As a result, just a glance from him would make me scared and wonder what I had done wrong. After I went to college, which was a great honor for the family, we started to have decent and pleasant conversations. One day we talked about his temper with my mother and sisters around. To my surprise, I realized that while my father admitted that it was his weakness, he actually felt proud of it.

Everyone loves themselves. A weakness, if they have it, may very well become something lovable. A strength, if they have it, will become the most important one for people to possess. People maintain their self-esteem simply by overvaluing the strength they have, by undervaluing the strength they do not have, by disregarding the weakness they have, and by believing their weakness is lovely. People have a primary focus on themselves, so how could anyone afford not loving themselves? It would be unbearable not to love him- or herself while an individual's primarily focus is on him- or herself.

Low self-esteem individuals just have weaker feeling of loving themselves in comparison to high self-esteem individuals. Low self-esteem individuals still love themselves. For a comprehensive review on how low self-esteem individuals perceive themselves, please see Tice, 1993.

Individuals with relatively low self-esteem are at high risk to a clinical depression (Tennen & Affleck,

1993). While the exact mechanism of how a clinical depression is developed is unknown, some individuals start to feel depressed simply because they feel that they are so lovable that they deserve more love and respect from others than they actually have obtained. They feel depressed about the fact that they have not gotten what they deserve.

Individuals affected by depression generally have a much stronger self-focus. If they could focus their attention away from themselves, they would not feel so depressed. If individuals do not love themselves at all, they would feel that they deserve any mishap in their lives. If they feel that they have gotten what they deserve, they would feel content. Some religions make people believe that they are here into this present life to experience torture either because of their past-life or to prepare a better after-life. They are taught to accept whatever happens to them. Those religions actually have prevented their believers from severe depressive reactions to misfortunes.

A common strategy people employ to ensure that they love themselves is to have positive illusions about themselves. You can conduct a simple experiment by asking people to assess how well they drive. If you ask people to describe themselves as either an above-average driver or an under-average driver, most likely you will find that about 80% of drivers think that they are above-average drivers. As you know, logically only 50% of individuals are above-average. Therefore, with regard to the strength of being a better driver, 30% of individuals have an illusion that they possess it while they actually do not. The majority of people believe they possess strengths of many areas that they actually do not possess. Those positive illusions about themselves are a major resource for people to maintain their self-esteem and their love for themselves. For a general discussion on positive illusions and their importance in maintaining psychological well-being, please see Taylor and Brown, 1988 &1994.

If we contest that there is absolutely no one who does not love themselves, it is probably too arbitrary. With the chance of one out of a thousand, if you happen to fall in love with a woman who really does not love herself, you will fail your seduction by using the strategy described in this chapter. It will be your luck to fail. A relationship with her will definitely make your life most miserable.

Since she initially loves herself the most, you can draw some attention from her if she feels that you are similar to her. You can draw more attention from her if she feels that you are more than her with those respects that have defined her. Your power to draw her attention away from herself depends on your reading of those respects by which she defines herself.

There are two types of characteristics in you that will be important to her. One group of characteristics comes from the social standard. In the process of socialization, certain characteristics that are considered important in society have been internalized in her mind to become important. Two most important examples are intelligence and beauty. Your intellectual level and your appearance certainly will be important aspects for drawing her attention away from her primary focus of herself. The second group of characteristics comes from her self-perception.

Among the strengths that she feels that she possesses (not necessarily that she really possesses), some may not be considered important at all in society. However, they are important when you try to draw her attention away as long as they are important to her for defining herself and for maintaining her self-esteem. For example, if she likes music, your ability to enjoy music will draw attention away from her self-focus. For me, because of my ability to write beautiful poems, being poetic has become my identity and one source of self-esteem, therefore, women who are artistic and poetic are appealing to me.

For many youngsters, the most instinctive way to try to attract women is showing off. It is in agreement with the conclusion that to attract her you need to make her feel that you are the top dog. However, it is very risky when showing off in an obvious way. Encountering someone who is better than themselves, people may react in two different ways. One is to compete and the other is to follow. Showing off can be perceived as a threat to her self-esteem. She has to do something about it. She can compete with you, find a way to belittle you, or avoid you to balance her psychological world. When you show off, your strength may become your enemy. You know what showing off is because when you show off you feel quite good about yourself at least for the moment. And she knows it too.

The best strategy is mirroring. You are her mirror. You need to start as the same as her. If she has a poetic soul, you show her that you have the very same soul. If she loves music, you show her that you love music to the same degree as she does. If she loves adventures, you show her that you love adventures to the same degree as she does. If she is good at math, you show her that you are good at math, too. If she is bad at math, for a safe play, you should not start to show her your math ability at the beginning.

First, you need to make her feel that you are just as good as she is in the respects by which she has defined herself. Then after a while, you may show her that you are a little bit better from time to time. When you are doing better, you need to convey the message that she could have done the same as well. Remember that you are her mirror image. A mirror image generally looks as good as the real thing and sometimes looks better with appropriate lighting. From time to time, you may want to make her feel that you are better than she is and that she is better than she feels she is.

Mirroring can also go to the feeling level. You may want to make her feel that you are feeling the same as she is in most situations. One way to achieve this is verbal empathy, which will be described in the next chapter. The other way is physical mirroring. In daily life, people consistently perceive and process nonverbal information without consciously knowing so. If you can mimic her nonverbally, she would feel that you are in the same mood with her and that you are staying with her emotionally. Specifically, after she changes her body position, you copy her body position after a while. If she puts her head on her right hand when she talks, you slowly put your head on your left hand, making your body position very similar to hers. Do not copy her immediately after she changes her position, though. Otherwise, she will realize that you are copying her intentionally.

Because she loves herself and because she primarily focuses her attention on herself, when she sees herself in you, she will allocate some of her attention to you. You, of course, will be different from her in many other ways, which makes you appear as an entity that is richer and broader than she is. In her psychological reality, you will gradually become a broader entity and she is part of it. You are the ocean and she a portion of the water in it. She then will feel that she belongs to you. Eventually, she loses herself in you.

Chapter Seven

The Feeling of Closeness

The feeling of closeness is fundamental for any close relationship. It is, of course, fundamental for romantic love. The closer she feels to you, the more likely romantic love is to develop. The mirroring strategy described in the previous chapter can certainly make her feel close to you. This chapter will discuss other strategies that can make her feel close to you.

Empathy is a key strategy that a therapist employs to build a positive therapeutic relationship. It has become the most basic strategy to be taught when new therapists or counselors are trained. Basically, you put yourself in her shoes. You feel whatever she feels when she is talking. Then you reflect back to her how she is feeling. For example, when she tells you about her conflict with her boss, if you sense that she feels mistreated, then you can say to her, "that's so unfair". She will feel that you have understood her and have accepted her. When she talks about a mistake she has made, you may say to her, "you must regret what you did … it was such a natural response in that situation". Anyway, you need to try and feel whatever she is feeling and convey back to her that you are feeling what she is feeling.

The key is, of course, that you do need to be able to feel what she is feeling. You can not just pretend that you do if you do not. We are all human beings. Our feelings are quite similar under similar circumstances. Therefore, her feelings most likely will be like yours if you are in her situation. Thus, it will be unlikely to get it wrong if you really pay attention to what she is talking about.

Sometimes you may miss some parts of her story, or she may fail to tell you some parts of her story, or she is just somehow different from you when responding to that particular situation. As a result, you may be wrong. In that case, as long as you are attentive and have conveyed to her that you are trying to understand her, she will try to explain to you how she really feels and why.

By interacting with her empathetically, you make her feel that she has been understood and accepted by you. People love themselves as I have discussed in the previous chapter. However, we often feel that we are the only ones who can really understand ourselves. When you show her that you can understand her and have understood her, she will be thrilled from the bottom of her heart. She likes that feeling and she will seek more. In the process of seeking empathy, understanding, and acceptance from you, she becomes the underdog. At the same time, she feels close to you.

People are lonely in nature. Many extroverted individuals feel lonely when they are alone and that is why they prefer to be around other people all the time. When they are with other people, they can forget their loneliness. Introverted individuals, on the other hand, actually have learned how to withstand loneliness better. The reason for loneliness is that people often find it is hard to find someone who can really understand them and accept them completely. A soul-mate is hard to find, as people say.

We love ourselves yet often we have doubts about ourselves. If she is the only one who loves herself, she may doubt that she is actually as lovable. If you can show her that you support her love for herself, she will feel at ease and less doubtful, and she will want to be close to you.

When we say that someone is a very close friend of ours, we use closeness to refer how good a relationship is. There are indices to assess how close a relationship really is. Most people use their feelings for their assessment. When they feel closeness, their assessment is that the relationship is a close one. It is not a bad index because feelings often tell the truth. However, very often our feelings can only tell us how we feel rather than how she feels. A more objective measure is the level of self-disclosure.

As a relationship grows closer, both individuals share more about themselves. How much information she shares with you, more specifically, how private the information she shares with you is indicates how close to you she feels. Personal information can be arranged along a dimension of "privateness". The more private information has been shared, the closer a relationship is. At the beginning of a relationship, people only talk about stuff that is public. "All we have talked about is the weather," some people may have complained about a bad relationship. As a relationship gets better, both people feel safer with each other and they will start to self-disclose some superficially private stuff.

Here is a guideline to assess how private some pieces of personal information are. The first level is attitudes and interests. She self-discloses her interests such as what she likes and what she does not. She also self-discloses her opinions on general topics such as politics, abortion, religion, and public figures. This is the first level of closeness and is generally the level when you start to call someone "a friend".

The second level is her relationships with someone you both know of or her relationship with her family members. Does she like, hate, or have conflicts with people you also have contact with? What happened? What is her relationship with her parents like? What kind of conflicts does she have with her parents? If she has self-disclosed this type of information, you can call her "a close friend".

The third level is her behaviors that are embarrassing. Those behaviors may not be acceptable by the current social standard or by her moral standard. If she tells you that she once stolen money from a roommate, and it is very unlikely that she would tell other people that, it indicates that she considers you as "a real close friend". If she tells you that she has masturbated, while imaging someone you both know of, most likely she considers you as "a real close friend".

There is also some personal information that people will never disclose to anyone. It is, therefore, the most private. The description above is just a rough classification. Each piece of personal information can have a different level of privateness in comparison to other piece of information. Individuals can have their own unique evaluations of how private a piece of personal information is.

Naturally, self-disclosure in a relationship is reciprocal. The levels of privateness of self-disclosure are generally very similar for the two people involved. It is the feeling of trust that determines how private people will go. When one person discloses information that is a little bit more private, the other person perceives it as a sign of trust from that person. The other person then will feel propelled to disclose information that reaches the same level of privateness to show his or her trust back. As the information becomes more private, more feelings of trust develop. This is a natural process of how the feeling of closeness develops.

If you want to earn her trust and closeness fast, you may try to go a little bit more private intentionally. As a result, she will go more private with you. If you gradually share more and more private personal information intentionally, you may develop a closer relationship with her intentionally. However, caution should be taken. If you go too private than she can accept and afford at the time being, she will be reluctant to go as private with you. If she does not like the pressure she feels, she may just stop interacting with you. This is, actually, one of the reasons why some people have a hard time making close friends. They simply disclose too much too soon and scare people away.

For a general discussion on empathy, please see Patterson, 1984. For a general discussion on self-disclosure, please see two excellent reviews by Collins and Miller (1994) and Enomoto (1983).

Chapter Eight

Activating the Constructs

Let's say Emily is going to a conference. Emily has a friend named Michelle. Michelle has told Emily that a male colleague of hers will also attend the conference. Michelle also has said that Emily and that man may be a good match. Suppose that Emily and that man have some limited contact during the conference. Let's assume that, under those circumstances, the possibility that Emily develops romantic feelings for that man is 5%.

Now let's suppose Emily does not have a friend Michelle and nothing has happened before the conference. Let's also suppose that Emily has the same amount of contact with that man. Under this new circumstance, the possibility that Emily develops romantic feelings for that man will be much less than 5%. What is the reason? In the first scenario, the construct of romance and love is primed to be more accessible in Emily's mind, whereas this is not the case in the second scenario.

People quite often get hooked up with their blind dates. If they had met the same person under different circumstances, they probably would not even have looked at each other twice. The reason is the same. In a blind date situation, constructs related to romantic love are primed and become more accessible to them. If you have done very well what has been discussed earlier in this book, it may have been enough for some people to develop romantic feelings for you. For others, however, you need to make efforts to make the constructs related to romantic love more accessible to them, especially as a response to your presence.

It is not rare that a man and a woman can be good friends for a long period of time, yet they have had a hard time developing romantic feelings. Very often, when one of them wants their relationship to go toward a romantic direction, the other person will be surprised because he or she has never thought it that way. Following are some different explanations for this scenario.

First, people are different in their accessibility to different constructs (Higgins, King, Mavin, 1982). For example, Michael tends to classify people as smart or stupid and classify behaviors as wise or foolish in all possible situations, while David tends to classify people or behaviors as masculine or feminine in all possible situations. That is, intelligence is an immediately accessible construct for Michael while gender is an immediately accessible construct for David.

Certain constructs are hard for some people to get access to in their mind. For example, some people may always judge others in terms of sexuality, whereas others may rarely judge people in that dimension. Facing the same situation, people who have different accessibility of constructs will perceive the situation differently, which may lead them to behave differently.

(By the way, when individuals perceive and behave differently in the same situation, we say that they have different personalities). There is an individual difference among people with regard to how accessible some constructs are. Constructs related to romantic love are easily accessible for some people yet they are hard to access for others.

Second, in some situations, many individuals do not have access to constructs related to romantic love. For example, two individuals can be very close colleagues. The primary context of contact is a working relationship and friendship. They may never have thought of developing a romantic relationship because the relationship is primarily defined and accepted as a working relationship and a friendship. Because of the primary definition, the concept of a love relationship is not the immediately accessible construct.

Third, some conditions prevent accessibility to constructs related to romantic love. For example, one person is married and the other is religiously or morally against love affairs outside a marriage. That is why many newlyweds have found that they are not as "popular" as when they were single. When an individual gets married, people around him or her would block their access to romantic constructs in relation to him or her.

To make her develop romantic love for you, you need to activate these constructs related to romantic love in her mind and make those constructs easily accessible for her. Telling her directly that you have feelings for her definitely opens the door for her to develop romantic feelings for you. However, if you do it before she has ever developed feelings for you and if your previous seduction work is not enough for her to willingly give it a try, you will lose your chance with her. Also, as will be discussed in later chapters, it is recommended not to express your feelings until she expresses her feelings for you clearly to avoid the pain of dealing with games in love relationships.

To activate some constructs in people's minds is not as hard as it appears. A completely unrelated task such as completing a sentence in which certain constructs are involved (e.g., "that boy argues with his mom a lot" for the construct of "disobedience") is proven to be able to activate that construct and influence people's perceptions on a later situation (If interested, please see Higgins, 1996 for a review). Therefore, occasionally talking about stuff related to romantic love will be enough to activate the construct. You can talk about a romantic movie you just saw, some rumors you heard about someone's romance, and practically everything that is related. When you have something to talk about, please remember to talk about it as if it is just a neutral topic and it is not related to your situation in any way.

Remember that your job is to activate her constructs and that your job is not to imply your interest in her. If she suspects that you have a specific intention when you bring up the topic, she may develop some resistance. A sentence like "last night I saw my friend and his girlfriend together", "my sister just got engaged", or "that's a very romantic painting" would be able to make the constructs related to romantic love more accessible.

There are many activities that can activate the construct of romantic love. However, some of them can not be done until some kind of relationship has been developed. If possible, try to engage in those activities. Those activities include: listening to romantic music together, taking a walk together in a quite night, going to a movie together, etc.

Some obstacles may prevent her from accessing to constructs related to romantic love. If so, you may want to dissipate them for her. If she perceives that it is impossible that you can ever be her lover, it will be hard for her to entertain any association between you and a romantic lover of hers. The most common example would be that you are in a romantic relationship with someone already. An extraordinary case would be that you are married and she perceives that you are very committed to your marriage.

To overcome this obstacle, some men try to hide the fact that they are married when earning a woman's love. Only after they have gotten her love, they tell her the fact of their marriage. When feeling the danger of losing her love, a man may start to tell lies, such as his marriage is a mess, his wife is a devil, and he is going to get a divorce. There are moral issues with regard to extramarital love affairs and deception, which is not a topic of this book. The aforementioned facts are just used to illustrate that obstacles need to be dissipated for romantic love to develop and grow. When there is an obstacle that makes her perceive you as inaccessible as a lover, you need to dissipate it for her romantic love to grow.

Chapter Nine
The Magic Behavior

There is an interesting dynamic of interpersonal interaction. One individual's certain type of behavior and action usually evokes certain type of reaction or response from the other individual who is involved in the interaction (Kiesler, 1983; Sullivan, 1953). For example, friendly-dominant behaviors most likely lead to docile and submissive behaviors. Unfriendly-dominant behaviors most likely lead to resistant behaviors and self-effacing feelings. In principle, when you behave in a way, you prescribe a group of behaviors to the other person whom you are interacting with. There might be some difference in individuals' reactions, depending on their personalities or past experiences. Most likely, however, people will take the prescription and behave in the prescribed role with some slight modifications.

Theoretically, there should be a set of behaviors that evokes feelings and behaviors that are related to romantic love. When that behavior is executed, the woman you are interacting with will behave as if she were your lover. If you know that behavior and execute that behavior repeatedly to a woman, she may very likely take the prescription and gradually develop feelings for you and behave as your romantic lover. I will call that behavior "the magic behavior".

Before describing the magic behavior, let's take a look at what people usually do when they interact with someone they have developed romantic feels for. Naturally, when a man loves a woman, he has a set of behaviors that is rooted in the fact that he has romantic feelings for her. I will call this behavior "the secondary behavior". When you love her, your behaviors are parallel to your feelings, even though you may not be intentionally doing so. The secondary behavior generally prescribes that she behaves nicely to you. The secondary behavior has a limited power to prescribe her a role as if she is your lover. Because of its power, people say that if you love her unconditionally and care for her consistently, she may love you back eventually. However, its power is limited. Because of the limitation of its power, it is very common that those you have fallen in love with do not love you, and at the same time, that those who have fallen in love with you may never earn your love.

The more powerful, magic behavior is the behavior that is rooted in the belief that she has romantic feelings for you. If you treat her as if she has romantic feelings for you, you prescribe a role for her to play and that role is the role of loving you romantically. When she repeatedly behaves in the prescribed role of loving you romantically, she will develop romantic love for you. As people say, if you treat someone as a friend, he or she will be your friend. If you treat someone as an enemy, he or she will be your enemy. Well, it turns out that, if you treat someone as your lover, he or she will be your lover.

When you treat someone as if you love her (i.e., execute the secondary behavior), the prescribed role is a role of being loved. The primary response of being loved is gratitude. As a result, she will behave nicely to you and not necessarily love you (although it is a possibility). On the other hand, when you treat her as if she romantically loves you (i.e., execute the magic behavior), the prescribed role is a role of loving you romantically. She will gradually adopt that role and develop romantic feelings for you.

To execute the powerful, magic behavior is easy. Just try to believe that she has romantic feelings for you and you will be executing the magic behavior automatically. Well, if you have done some of what we have discussed in the previous chapters, she may very likely have romantic feelings for you already. Just tell yourself that she has romantic feelings for you before you meet her the next time, and each time thereafter.

Two cautions need to be discussed here. First, do not assume that she is madly in love with you already, especially at the beginning. Otherwise, your prescription would be a mission-impossible for her. Very likely, she would feel that you behave in a ridiculously weird way. Second, do not confuse love with sex. It is very easy for most women to tell the difference between romantic love and pure sexual attention. While most women welcome love, only a few women enjoy pure sexual attention. Unwanted sexual attention can be very annoying for many women. Men, on the other hand, tend to welcome both.

The difference between romantic love and pure sexual attention can be easily understood from a man's point of view. It is love when you tell yourself "such a wonderful woman deserves the most wonderful life and I hope that I can be the one who makes her happy". It is sexual attention when you tell yourself "I would enjoy having sex with such a sexy woman and I want her badly". While romantic love relationship often involves sex, for most women the affection part

71

of a love relationship is easier to accept than the sex part, especially at the beginning. Therefore, when you execute the magic behavior, be careful not to treat her too much as if she wants to have sex with you. Also, if you prefer to execute the secondary behavior, treat her as you love her rather than as you want her.

There is a common mistake for men when they pursue a relationship with a woman. Many men feel that how much sexual contact is allowed is an indicator of how much a woman is in love with them. As a result, they try very hard to get more sexual contact than a woman is ready for. A woman may give in, but if she does not feel enough affection to support those sexual behaviors, she may wonder if it is sex that you really want rather than a love relationship. Sex without affection upsets many women because they feel that they are just your sexual objects, which makes them feel no different from a prostitute.

Chapter Ten

Women's Game

For an ideal seduction, it is highly recommended to follow the procedure outlined in Chapter One. Many people cannot wait until she expresses her feelings first. One of the reasons is that they run out of patience. They feel that they have done everything and she should be expressing by now. The other reason is that they have started the process of seduction too late. They have fallen too much in love before they start. As a result, the feeling inside them is just too strong to hold any longer. In either case, it is highly advised against breaking the procedure by expressing your feelings before she does.

Under certain circumstances, however, it is impossible to follow the procedure. For example, she is leaving town permanently and there will be no way to complete the seduction procedure before she is gone. When the procedure is not followed completely, when you express your feelings directly to her before she expresses hers, most likely you will have to deal with games people play when starting and maintaining romantic relationships. It will make the experience far less enjoyable. Many men find that it is hard and annoying to identify and deal with games women play in their love experiences. Some women find that men play games, too. Men play similar games, just to a lesser extent. The difference between men and women will be explained later.

To understand how and why women play games, our discussion will start with a client of mine. A young man expressed his romantic feelings to my female client. She rejected him. Two weeks later, he started to date one of her roommates. One week after they started dating, my client went into a deep depression. She was accompanied by her friend (another roommate of hers) to my office, asking for help.

A careful examination found that she had several depressive symptoms and occasional suicidal thoughts. She expressed feelings of low self-worth and high self-doubts. Those symptoms were exactly the same as the symptoms in women who were dumped by their long-term boyfriends. A careful discussion with my client found no evidence that she was actually interested in the young man when she rejected him. The roommate who accompanied her to my office was a very close friend of my client. A talk with the friend completely confirmed the fact that she was not purposefully playing hard-to-get with the young man when she rejected him.

For many men, it is very hard to understand my client's reaction to the situation. If she did not have feelings for that young man, whatever he did should not bother her. If she had a big heart, she should have been happy for him because the young man had found happiness that she could not give. If she hated the young man's conduct (i.e., his quick change of feelings), she should have felt good that she had made a right decision not to let the young man be part of her life. It seemed that she had no reason to be depressed. If you tell this story to women, however, most of them will feel sympathetic to my client.

Women's psychological world is somehow different from men's. Very often, when a man feels a woman is playing games, the woman actually has no obvious intention of playing any game at all. Rather, what they are doing is their natural reaction under certain circumstances. Their behaviors are well based on the principles of their psychological world.

Only a few women intentionally play games in romantic relationships. Those women also are motivated by their natural needs. If you can understand what need motivates their games, you will not blame them as well. However, for many men, perceiving that a woman whom they have fallen in love with is playing games with them naturally evokes negative feelings. It is very hard to deal with games when you do not have a good understanding of the root of the games.

A little discussion about women seems necessary here to understand why and how they play games. As we have discussed in the previous chapters, individuals' feelings of self-worth is of central importance in maintaining their feelings of happiness and in maintaining their daily living. After adolescence, people started to receive offers of romantic love. Offers of romantic love that an individual has received are a very important source in support of men's and women's feelings of their self-worth. In comparison to men, women use offers of romantic love to support their feelings of self-worth to a much more extent. For men, in comparison to women, other sources (academic achievements, knowledge of sports, etc.) have a greater importance in support of their feelings of self-worth.

That is, offers of romantic love are a rather primary source in support of women's feelings of self-worth. On the other hand, offers of romantic love are one of several sources in support of men's feelings of self-worth. If offers of romantic love provide 85% of the total support for women's feelings of self-worth, they probably provide about 50% of the total support for men's feelings of self-worth. As will be discussed later, games people play are typically rooted in their feelings of self-worth. Therefore, men play games to a lesser extent than women do.

Now, my client's reaction is quite easy to understand. When the young man expressed his feelings to her, his offer of romantic love became one important source to support her feeling of self-worth. That source of support was naturally expected to last for a relatively long period of time. The young man's dating of her roommate in such a short period of time was very unusual. Her psychological schema was unprepared for this unexpected total withdrawal of this important source that supported her feeling of self-worth. Her feeling of self-worth, therefore, was suddenly faced with danger. Unable to cope with this danger, her feeling of self-worth had become unsupported and disarrayed. It then collapsed. As a result, depressive symptoms developed. This client's reaction was quite severe. However, if were faced with this unusual situation, most women would react in the same way, possibly to a lesser extent.

Offers of romantic love are like treasure stones in women's pocket. Whenever they receive an offer of romantic love, they put that treasure stone in their pocket. After starting their pursuit by expressing their feelings, many men continuously make efforts after the first rejection, which will make the treasure stone safely stay in the woman's pocket with a consistent or even increasing value. However, it will not do much good for a man who wants to be romantically loved back. There is only a very slight chance that a woman would be so touched by a man's persistence and would develop romantic feelings for him. Persistent asking to be loved back, which is very likely to make a man a beggar, eventually will make the woman feel annoyed. There is even a good chance that a feeling of disdain can be evoked by consistent begging. No romantic love can ever be possible then.

A better strategy is to have a feigned withdrawal shortly after you are rejected. It will maximize your chance of success (although the chance is still small). A feigned withdrawal will not cost you anything because you can always restart your direct pursuit if that is your style. There are two reasons for making a feigned withdrawal. First, if she has some amount of feelings for you, she will try to have you back instead of throwing all of them away. Second, your offer of romantic love has become a treasure stone in her pocket and it is expected to stay there. If you take it away from her pocket, she will try to take it back (consciously or subconsciously). When you make the feigned withdrawal, you should not take it away completely, as the young man did to my client. My client did not make any effort to take the stone back because she felt that it had become impossible. How valuable your stone is to her determines how much effort she will make to put it back into her pocket. If she has enough treasure stones already, if the ability to attract you is not deemed valuable (e.g., she feels that you are an under- underdog to her), not much effort will be made.

A feigned withdrawal can be made by sending a clear message that you respect her choice and that you are almost in control of your feelings already. You can quietly observe her reaction within a couple of days. Most likely she will give you some clue that she is interested in you. When her behavior is inviting, you need to grasp the opportunity. If she wants you back to pursue her, most likely she has certain good feelings for you. She is, at the same time, willing to open the door to see if those good feelings can turn into romantic feelings.

Even if her invitation is totally due to her love of your treasure stone, there is still a mechanism that romantic love may develop. To get her treasure stone back, she is trying to attract you back to pursue her. A discrepancy exists in her psychological world. She is making efforts to invite you to pursue her, and yet, she has no romantic feelings for you. Her behavior and her feeling are, therefore, incongruent. When individuals have obvious discrepancies in their psychological schemata, they need to resolve it. It is consciously or subconsciously uncomfortable when discrepancies exist. According to a psychological principle (Festinger, 1957), the discrepancy in her psychological schema will be resolved either by changing her inviting behavior or by developing romantic feelings for you.

Chapter Eleven
When the Moment Comes

Many people consider that inviting behavior after giving a rejection is the well-known hard-to-get game. As discussed in the previous chapter, in most situations, it is just a natural process that is not intentionally designed at all.

Games people play typically stem from their feelings of self-worth. Some women believe that men who get them easily will not treasure them. Intentional hard-to-get players believe that they are just making an effort to ensure being treasured in the future. They believe that their intentional play of hard-to-get has nothing to do with their feelings of self-worth.

However, a boost to their feelings of self-worth is at least a secondary gain for them. After all, if they had sufficient feelings of self-worth, they probably would not feel the need to manipulate their prices.

Charm-testing is another game that is directly associated with individuals' feelings of self-worth. People play it whenever they feel the need to assure their charm. For some, an appreciative look is enough. For others, they want you to tell them that you love them. A client of mine, for example, was a young college graduate who worked in a bank. He found that a young woman had been flirting with him lately. He wanted to start a relationship with her and asked her for a romantic relationship. She rejected him and told him that she had a boyfriend. He directly pursued her for two weeks and then backed off. Two months later, he reported that she started to play cute with him again. Then he learned from other source that she had a good relationship with her boyfriend and had gotten engaged a month ago. This turned out to be a classic charm-testing case. When she started to flirt with him, it was to confirm that she was still charming. Especially when a long-term relationship has lasted for a while, some people have a need to test their charm elsewhere. An offer of romantic love with some persistence generally completes the test. It is atypical that the young woman tried a retest with the new college graduate. Probably the first test was not very satisfactory for her because he had backed off easily. Although there was a slim chance that they might end up spending one or two romantic nights together if the young man handled the situation well, a long-term love relationship was quite impossible.

Under certain conditions, it is a natural process for an individual to play games. It is not a bad behavior to be blamed. However, games can be really confusing and frustrating to deal with. If you continue your seduction until she clearly expresses her feelings to you, you will minimize the chance of dealing with her games directly. Before she makes that big step of expressing her feelings, most of the issues related to her feelings of self-worth have to be resolved inside her mind. After she expresses her feelings to you, even if you have to deal with a game or two, it will be less confusing and less frustrating because now you know that she romantically loves you.

A clear expression of her feelings is not necessarily a verbal statement. It can be nonverbal. But it must have an unambiguous meaning. Be careful about your wishful thinking. Individuals often interpret an ambiguous action in a way that entertains what they have been wishing for. Although it is not easy, you need to resist your urge to express your feelings directly before she does.

Sometimes, it can be very tempting to just tell her how you feel about her. For example, she may say to you, "Jim told me that he has feelings for me. What do you think?" She probably is trying to push you to tell her that you want to have a relationship with her as well. However, it should not be interpreted as meaning that she'd rather be with you, which wishfully satisfies the requirement of an expression of feelings from her. If you start to express your feelings to her at this point, you vulnerably make yourself one of the two from whom she has the right to choose. You may want to tempt her a little, "It seems like you have someone else in mind."

In the procedure outlined in Chapter One, it is recommended to accept her love immediately. First, it is the only way that is fair. It takes a lot of courage for individuals to express their romantic feelings first, which puts them in a vulnerable position. It takes even more for a woman to express her romantic feelings first because traditionally women are not hunters for romantic love. In tradition, women typically wait for their princes to come to them. If you love her, you should not make her suffer. Second, rejection or reluctance in accepting an offer of romantic love sometimes may close the door completely. After rejection, if she is overwhelmed by her feelings of being an under-underdog, she may not make any further effort. For some individuals, even if you start to pursue them directly, they may not give you a chance any more because they feel that they have been hurt too much. People are afraid of being hurt in a relationship. By rejecting her, you have hurt her already before the relationship even starts. Third, reluctance in accepting a woman's offer of romantic love puts doubts in her mind about you and the relationship. She may consistently wonder about what she has gotten into. You can not fully enjoy a romantic love if she can not fully enjoy it. Reluctance in accepting a man's offer of romantic love, on the other hand, less likely puts doubts in his mind. When they have finally "conquered" their "prey" after the initial rejection, some men may have a short-lived feeling of a boosted self-esteem.

As we have discussed, while leading her develop romantic feelings for you, you lead her feel that she is the underdog. If her romantic feelings for you are too strong to hold any longer, she will eventually express her feelings to you. However, feeling as the underdog, she may have worries. She wonders if you will accept her romantic love for you if she expresses. Therefore, you may want to foster a psychological environment in which she feels safe with you. You need to tell yourself that you are ready to accept her love at any moment. She will get this message from you and feel safe with you.

Your physical environment is also important. When individuals look at something appealing (e.g., a picture of their children, a charming face), their pupils become larger. When individuals look at something they do not like, on the other hand, their pupils become smaller (Hess, 1965). Therefore, larger pupils are associated with positive affections, whereas smaller pupils are associated with negative affections. At the same time, people's pupils are also affected by light. People's pupils become smaller in strong light and become larger in weak light. Lovers prefer to go out at night. At night, people's pupils become larger due to the weak light. When lovers look at each other's eyes and see the larger pupils, they feel as if the other person is more affectionate toward them than they really are. That is why night appears more romantic.

It is, therefore, advised to always avoid facing a source of bright light when you are with her. When you face direct light, your pupils become smaller. When she sees your smaller pupil, she can not feel the love and acceptance from you. If your pupils are larger, on the other hand, she will feel that you have strong affection for her.

When the moment comes, you will be ready. You have had romantic feelings for her for so long. This is the moment you have been waiting for. You are so excited. She looks at you. She feels your affection for her. She expresses her feelings to you. Immediately, you express your feelings to her.

An immediate acceptance that is handled well makes your romantic love look like a mutual development, where both of you express your feelings to each other at the same time. It is a natural development when both individuals have made efforts and when both individuals have wanted a romantic relationship with each other. A romantic love, when perceived as having developed naturally, mutually, and as if it was fated, will bring the most enjoyment and the fewest problems to a relationship.

References

Collins, N. L., & Miller, L. C. (1994). Self-disclosure and liking: A meta-analytic review. *Psychological Bulletin, 116,* 457-475.

Enomoto, H. (1983). A review of studies on self-disclosure as an interpersonal exchange. *Japanese Psychological Review, 26,* 148-164.

Festinger, L. (1957). *A theory of cognitive dissonance.* Evanston, IL: Row, Peterson.

Hess, E. H. (1965). Attitude and pupil size. *Scientific American, 212,* 46-54.

Higgins, E. T. (1996). Knowledge activation: Accessibility, applicability, and salience. In E. T. Huggins and A. W. Kruglanski (Eds.),

Social psychology: Handbook of basic principles (pp. 133-168). New York: Guilford Press.

Higgins, E. T., King, G. A. & Marvin, G. H. (1982). Individual construct accessibility and subjective impressions and recall. *Journal of Personality and Social Psychology, 43,* 35-47.

Kiesler, D. J. (1983). The 1982 Interpersonal Circle: A taxonomy for complementarity in human transactions. *Psychological Review, 90,* 185-214.

Patterson, C. H. (1984). Empathy, warmth, and genuineness in psychotherapy: A review of reviews. *Psychotherapy: Theory, Research, Practice, Training, 21,* 431-438.

Sullivan, H. S. (1953*). The interpersonal theory of psychiatry*. New York: Norton.

Taylor, S. E., & Brown, J. D. (1988). Illusion and well-being: A social psychological perspective on mental health. *Psychological Bulletin, 103,* 193-210.

Taylor, S. E., & Brown, J. D. (1994). Positive illusion and well-being revisited: Separating fact from fiction. *Psychological Bulletin, 116,* 21-27.

Tennen, H., & Affleck (1993). The Puzzle of self-esteem: A clinical perspective. In R. F. Baumeister (Ed.), *Self-esteem: The puzzle of low self-regard* (pp. 241-262). New York: Plenum.

Tice, D. M. (1993). The social motivation of people with low self-esteem. In R. F. Baumeister (Ed.), *Self-esteem: The puzzle of low self-regard* (pp. 37-53). New York: Plenum.